HOUSE WITH

THE BLUE

BED

mercury house san francisco

HOUSE WITH THE BLUE BED

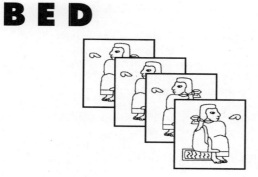

BY

ALFRED ARTEAGA

Published in the United States of America by Mercury House,
San Francisco, California, a nonprofit publishing company
devoted to the free exchange of ideas and guided by a
dedication to literary values.

United States Constitution, First Amendment: Congress shall
make no law respecting an establishment of religion, or
prohibiting the free exercise thereof; or abridging the
freedom of speech, or of the press; or the right
of the people peaceably to assemble,
and to petition the Government
for a redress of grievances.

Mercury House and colophon are registered trademarks of
Mercury House, Incorporated.

Printed in Canada on acid-free paper.

Library of Congress Cataloguing-in-Publication Data:
Arteaga, Alfred, 1950–
House with the blue bed / by Alfred Arteaga.
p.   cm.
isbn 1-56279-106-0 (alk. paper)
1. Arteaga, Alfred, 1950– —Journeys. 2. Poets,
American—20th century—Biography. 3. Mexican
Americans—Biography. 4. Voyages and travels.
5. Poetry—Authorship. I. Title.
ps3551.r726z465   1997
811'.54—dc21   97-26875

cip

9 8 7 6 5 4 3 2 1
first edition

para
Marisol
hija mía

Contents

HOUSE WITH THE BLUE BED

Blood, Sand, Blood

for kyf

A perfect walk up from the water
round Mullaghmore, the little boats
becoming more so, shrink
in view then wait in memory
behind the hill. Tomorrow Bundoran
or Lissadell, it makes such little difference,
we'll walk about the same, and this
bright light can neither repeat nor fade.
Though pleasure craft may diminish and finally
sink from view, though I sweat, you slow,
we are the distant sinking's fiery glow.

sand

There is no sand like this anywhere else. The steps themselves lose themselves at each step, not the trace, for I sink nearly to my knee at each step and leave a trail of deep tracks, but the trajectory of step is lost in the act of each puncture I make in such sand. What is lost and what remains, or perhaps the better question I raise remembering walking there beside the North Atlantic has nothing to do with recalling the original action, but is simply, what do I make now as memory of something lost?

It is summer sand, summer on Donegal Bay, or Bá Dhún na nGall, as it is untranslated in the Irish, halfway and walking distance between Streedagh and Mullaghmore. Streedagh is where ships lost from the Armada washed up, where Spaniards were eaten by the Irish, as the locals like to say. Mullaghmore is where Mountbatten was killed by an IRA blast. The sand has a consistency something like cake frosting that has been allowed to sit: its surface is smooth, stiff, almost hard but extremely thin. The pressure of any human foot breaks through to the most loosely packed, aerated interior. Each step forgets its forward trajectory and succumbs to a flash of panic that comes from the strength and very weakness of the step. Our feet walk not so much confidently as they do relatively ignorant, disinterested in our trail of steps yet jerked to reaction at the trip, stub, twist, or sudden plunge.

6

sand

It is sand like no other I've encountered I am sure. The broad beach peels back from the Bay and North Atlantic across from Dernish, the tiny island where Dermot wanted to buy one of the two houses but settled instead on Loughaun, the eroding point, which is gradually becoming island. Facing the open bay and sea beyond, the beach is sharp in its rise from the water, the sand, a steep angle for a couple of meters before it flattens out in the wide beach. It is a warm sand, the summer of the decade, it had been declared over and again, yet the water cooler there than at Streedagh or Lissadell or Rosses Point.

That sand deceives by a firmness, its surface, that belies a soft interior. It is a broad beach between two points of violent history just minutes in Co Sligo from Counties Leitrim and Donegal and from Co Fermanagh, the westernmost of Northern Ireland. It is a firm surface of memory, steps across a sand between the Irish Republic and the United Kingdom, deceiving in its appearance and first tentative touch. No one can walk its skin, any human foot would break through, and at each breaking, a sense of direction is lost, the purpose of the step shaken off in the surprise of the break. The skin is warmer than the interior beneath; it is the reverse of the human body, than the skin and blood of the foot, for example. I recall walking there, losing steps there, as in no other place. In truth I lost my way coming aware of each single step.

7

sand

 **sands**

The sand on Galveston is very fine. I have spent almost as much time walking that beach on the Gulf of Mexico as I have spent stepping into the Irish beach halfway between Streedagh and Mullaghmore, that is, very little time. Galveston is flatter than Ireland, and if it weren't that it is surrounded by water, I imagine I could smack a cue ball on Galveston grass and knock an eight ball into a corner pocket in Houston. On the gulf side, tiny ripples break, imitate waves, with crests of moss-colored foam, colored by the film of free petroleum. The sand itself approaches powder and could rightly be called so were it not for the humidity.

But the Galveston sand itself means next to nothing to me. It is a sand of little consequence that occurs to me after considering a walk in Co Sligo, each step as deep as it was forward. Then, I pause, what is it of Galveston that asserts its presence before my mind's eye, memory and heart, what that asserts presence after recalling that Irish beach? There is the link, sand to sand, beach to beach, clearly, an echo, mirror or repetition of course, but just as soon and as likely, it is a step not taken: Galveston fades from my memory, pale as an afterthought, as soon as presence, a potential here for consideration, manifests, the sands of Galveston fade or are rejected or perhaps even, are aborted before proper formation.

There are as many other images that could arise after the Irish steps other than the Texan as there are stars yet unseen in the night sky. Why the Gulf of Mexico after the North Atlantic? Why indeed. Why not instead, or even now replacing the vision of Galveston sands, the impossibility of movement on the Angel tube platform or fleeing tear gas and the police off Whittier Boulevard or the letter never posted to Megève? *What,* I say, is a primary question of human thought, and I ask, *what is next?* And in parallel I wonder, *what instead?* Or simply, *what not?*

As such I am as easily again at the Irish seashore considering once again a sand I have never conceived before. With the write of the poet, seeing a sand once again that I have never seen before. It is a sand of most fragile surface; it skirts the lip of the ocean, and it is profound. My tracks behind me mark a clear path to my present site and state, of this I have little doubt. Before me an unbroken plane of surface, sand I could track across, in posse, and in esse in my imagination and space and time. I stand up to my knees in sand; I cannot see my feet, cool below the fragile surface somewhere below, somehow oddly not present. They are not on the plane of my tracks, on the plane of the surface of the warm and easily ruptured sand beside the North Atlantic on a hot summer, Irish day. What track, what step in the sand, next? What rupture of surface, what depth instead?

This is then what occurs to me next, now at this juncture, instead of a repetition of walks and beaches north and south: *what next? what instead?* I have begun this literal excursion with a simple walk in Ireland, and its presence as starting point forever colors what becomes present here after it and more particularly what what comes to be. Rather, at this moment, than follow the path across the sand or from sand to other sand, and even rather than consider what lies beneath the surface plane, that is, rather than direction and alternation, than linear movement and selective identification, than horizontal and vertical, rather than these, the matter of *rather* itself. Each step forward breaks a surface to some other. The Irish sand of fragile surface and profound depth is the point I begin again and again, both as a first time and as subsequent motion on a prescribed path. This is where I begin now, once again, present in the present, about to step and about to redefine my path. I begin then with a walk across Irish sand on a hot summer day. I begin not with the material matter there, but with the steps and the possibility of sand.

3 air

So what if the better part of a year has passed this rainy day late spring in Berkeley and as I look out it is toward the bay and the pacific beyond, which I cannot see for the dense gray fog, but that I believe is there? What does it mean to write and to conceive now and here, obscured from the sea, its cold water, its dark sand, once again my steps across a fragile surface? Is it a plain break in logic, a lie, or perhaps a falling from the span and order of time? Or is it merely the play of language set in motion by a lyric sensibility?

Straight inland from the beach, at the distance of a long walk (for what isn't walking distance in Ireland?), juts up from the brown plane of bog, green hay field, and slate-blue lough Ben Bulben, the broad, flat mountain that is the center of local reckoning and most commanding of landmarks in Yeats's country. I found myself at the foot of Ben Bulben late, late one night, some days after the St. John's Eve fires of Sligo and Donegal, and yet other days before the death of the young boy felled by a tractor in Ballyconnell. It was after midnight, heading toward 3 am, and the sky was full of deep red folds and reddish violet and cold deep blue; such a wonder, something never seen by me or by any of my ancestors, native as we are to Mesoamerica and Iberia, too far south to witness such a night sky.

We were a small group, five in all: the kind poet who had just gotten money from the organization with stars on a blue field to write a screenplay in Irish; her son, the composer, a modern who wrote atonal; the hotel manager, at whose house we found ourselves, whose American wife had gone off for days, with a woman we imagined; the lost piano teacher, the only one that night I couldn't take my mind off; and five, me.

The land in from the sea to Ben Bulben is level, not flat, but level. There is variation, such as bogs where who knows what might be interred, preserved; slight surface undulations called hills, fields and breaks in the fields called roads. There is nothing till Ben Bulben to stop the wind. It is the north North Atlantic after all, and air might as naturally emanate from the polar ice cap or Ellesmere Island as it might from Galveston and the warming zone of the gulf stream, even midsummer. But regardless of the source, its point of origin and thus its definition, for winds after all are

air

named for their compass point source, nothing so much as unsettles the flow of wind until it comes against the broad and flat-topped mountain.

The hotel manager was hurting, that's certain, but took us into his home, gave us wine, and disappeared to barbecue salmon outdoors beneath the northern sky palette coming on 3 am. The poet drank befitting an Irish poet and drank more. She loved her son, that was evident, and managed to remain just enough of a conversant so as to prevent the two musicians from falling out, from condescension on the one hand and resentment on the other. The composer spoke to me about the kind of music Lyn Hejinian's husband does in San Francisco, in a vocabulary and syntax largely unknown to me. In the end, his speaking for the avant garde put me off; I think he had spent too much time in England.

The piano teacher was lost, small, and, by Irish standards, brown. Both she and I were at the mercy of the car owners: kind poet and sad hotelier. We had wanted to spend time alone together before she went back to her husband and I to my daughters. So we exited the house out the American-style sliding glass doors, I think Stan Getz was on the machine, out into the brilliant night sky and a senseless wind.

This is the point of evoking this memory: that wind. Stepping out of that house should have been into black. As we faced out to the sea there were no

15

air

artificial lights before us, but there was the northern night sky. It was cool, a cool night but not cold, and the air was full of the sea, unimpeded in its rush east, in its rush across the mostly liquid undulating surface of the North Atlantic, across the mostly solid undulations of Co Sligo up to this point, to the very point the lost, small, and brown piano teacher and I stood, at the foot of Ben Bulben.

The wind broke up: were it personified it could be felt to panic, dazed. It lost its clear trajectory, breaking up into synecdoches of wind, purposeless and wild at the collision with the mountain. We stood at this surprise, winds coming at us from every direction: our hair, her dress, blown back and forth consecutively and back and forth and every which way all at once. This is the point: standing there with my back to Ben Bulben, next to the lost piano teacher, facing the sea, at the break up of the invisible but real push from the sea, in the chaos of simultaneous and multiple impulse, there I was alive that moment and I am alive this moment yet these two moments do not equate. Standing there not taking a step I, in a small way like the mountain, made chaos, broke the flow of air from the sea in fragments like meaning.

air

4 breath

In a late second millennium consideration of meaning in verse, Charles Olson focused on the air of meaning and a machine of writing. The typewriter, it seems, in its uniform progression of letter, space, and punctuation, could accurately register the pace of the poet, the flow of phrase, the beat of breath. Today, at the transition from that millennium to the next, I compose music with the help of several electronic machines. The notes I play are written to the staff as I play them, but being as I am human, my sequencing software offers me the ability to overcome that. I simply accept its offer to quantize and my flesh and blood sense of rhythm is digitized, each note is precisely placed on a temporal grid, each approaching perfect duration.

The differences between Olson's typewriter and my synthesizer and sequencer don't interest me at this point, nor do the differences between poet's breath and musician's fingering. Instead I am interested in a similarity, in an underlying assumption of both, in a faith in the projection of meaning across time. In a fundamental sense, I think Olson's typed text and my musical score project a syntax, an order for reading that imagines or tries to represent a passage across time. Perhaps this is more evident in the music: the staff indicates pitch vertically and indicates tempo, the beat over time, horizontally. That is, music is written from left to right, in an order of notes that implies a succession of sounds across a span of time. To quantize that succession is to regularize intervals according to an accurate and electronic clock. Olson's typed text, in its uniform succession, its indications of letter, space, punctuation, the very syllables' voicing and inhaling and exhaling, implies a similar succession across time. Neither notes nor syllables are written all at once or in chaotic fashion; they peel off in order, in a sequence construed not only in order but in time. The uniformity of the typewriter and the quantizing of the sequencer function similarly; they regularize a pace of meaning (syllable or note) over a span of time, whether it is the human time of breaths or electronic time of seconds.

But lest the quantizing make the electronic music too machine like, the sequencer also offers the opportunity to humanize, that is, to introduce error in the fixing of beat to clock and so imitate the human, imprecise flow and ebb of beat and rest.

breath

5 **bodies**

There are three instances of the human body at rest that seem to me moments when immobility forced a reconsideration of what it is to act human. The instances are three occurrences I witnessed, three moments of local crisis, scattered in disparate locales, drawn together here in my text one after the other in a reading of difference.

I was browsing in Waterstone's bookstore when I heard the sharp protest of an automobile straining to stop, a long shriek of brakes. I have lived urban enough not to react instantly and uncooly to the sudden, be it a racial slur, or as in this case, a distant commotion on the street, so that by the time I did walk out, a crowd had already gathered on Earl's Court Road.

There in the street, neat against the English kerb, lay a woman in her own blood. She seemed calm, awake, and reminded me, perhaps because of her hair, of Ophelia in Millais's painting, even though she did not hold her arms outstretched but rather before her, hands clasped as if in prayer. But they were not in prayer but clasping the hand of a young man crouched beside her. He said nothing; she said nothing. It appeared as if they had been strangers just moments prior. Traffic was stopped; people gathered slowly.

In the middle of the street, from about twenty meters away, came a woman with Ophelia's shoe. What else was there to do? The young man clutching her hand gave the broken woman the most that any of us could, in silence and in touch and in confirmation that he would be for her what she could no longer be for herself. All that was left was to retrieve the shoe, and the woman's approach meant that even the trivial too would be taken care of; there was no need for Ophelia to move.

Some time after this, at the most a few months, I found myself in Paris, at the top of a seven-story walk-up, in a room whose windows looked out the mansard roof, trying to dial the telephone. The phone was broken in a most interesting and vexing sort of way: it would dial only reluctantly and then without sound. I did not hear the car this time but was called to the window by deep cries of pain.

There in the street stories below lay a woman writhing in a small clearing between the French cars. She lay writhing, on her elbows, shifting left then right. She wore blue jeans, one leg of which bent in an impossible angle. She cried out loudly, deep, throaty, as if for cries she had sampled the roars from the lion house at the San Francisco Zoo.

Beside her was a taxi, the taxi that broke her walk on the avenue des Gobelins. The driver was a dark man, what goes for Arabe in Paris. A pale man emerged from another car, yelled at the driver and in a most French way, slapped him. The pale man must have needed to do something, driven as he was by the woman's inability to get up and by her growls in primal French.

Much later, perhaps two years, I was at home in San José and for no particular reason approached the front window. There in the street before my house were three Mexicans, two men and a boy, Mexicans rather than Chicanos I would say because of their dress, though they could well have been Texanos. One man stood with the slight sway of a drunk, his hand pulled by the boy in a gesture that was perhaps familiar to the son. On the pavement before them in a bright red shirt lay a very still, very dark man. The standing man called to the still one; the boy seemed anxious to act some good.

Suddenly a navy blue–and–white San José PD car pulled up, carrying in it two of the same uniformed types that would make my daughter kneel before them and hold a gun to her head just a short time in the future and just a few houses down the street. Instantly the drunk Mexican panicked and tried to walk away; the boy, less afraid, hesitated. The two policemen got out of the car, grabbed the drunk Mexican, handcuffed him, and pushed him into the back seat of the car. They said something to the boy I could not hear; he took off frightened.

22

It was only then that they turned to the fallen man. He remained face down, motionless. The police made no effort to examine the fallen man but handcuffed him immediately. They picked up the body by its hands and dragged it to the curb, face in the gutter, legs stretched at a right angle into the street. Having done that they got on the radio for the paramedics.

bodies

6 rape

Shortly after first becoming a father, I returned to Los Angeles from New York with new baby daughter and wife. It was about the time I turned 24, and the father/husband/family thing seemed yet new and awkward. The three of us stayed with my sister and her husband, sleeping on the floor of their apartment in Silverlake, near the park where John Lennon would go.

I was jerked awake in the night or early morning black by screams. I was dazed and filled with fear: where was I? what was going on? And then most importantly, were my child and wife safe? After an eternity of seconds I made sense: I was at my sister's; we were safe. Then I heard a car come to life in the distance and speed away in escape. None but me in the apartment had awakened. I then heard a neighbor's door open, and steps took off to do something.

The screaming woman had been raped. The neighbor had rushed to her far too late; even the cries had come after the rapist had fled. For moments in the dark I had tried to sort things, to establish what was what and then act. But it had all been too late; even the screams, the live screams, were a record of a violence past.

24

rape

7 days

When I separated from my wife I returned once again to Los Angeles, this time from the San Francisco Bay area, from a house in San José and a job in Berkeley. I had Rockefeller money to spend a year at UCLA and write a book about time. I found myself in the city of my birth yet severed from family and home. And almost as disorienting, I found myself living in Westwood.

I think the fact of Westwood is not an insignificant factor in an affliction I acquired, which I came to call *dislocasia*. The disorientation I often felt upon waking, in the dizzy transition from sleep, came to be for me, rather than a transition, a lifestyle. For Westwood, that section of Los Angeles at the base of UCLA, Bel Air and Beverly Hills, between Hollywood and Santa Monica, strikes me as in essence off. And it isn't the matter of simulacra, the late twentieth-century dis-topos of philosophy that construes Los Angeles the great postmodern affair. I was born midcentury in the City of Angels, the simulacrum is home, and I can work up no particular awe for Hollywood, Disneyland or the Bonaventure, whether it be late capitalist, French, or paparazzi. It is the realness of Westwood that so managed to spin me hopelessly into confusion.

I was in B. Dalton Books on Westwood Blvd looking, I think, for some continuity from books, cleaved as I was from family and home in separation en route to divorce. After all, I seemed the same in bookstores, regardless whether they were in Bloomsbury or Westwood, and despite my fascination at their differences, the preponderance of Faber *&* Faber books, the methods of organization, the different magazines, I, nevertheless, seemed to myself about the same in each location, undertaking similar motions and expending similar time. I entered the bookstore from the LA winter of Westwood, a good summer for most places, simply to kill time. I lived on Levering, in Westwood, not so much walking as spitting distance from the cinemas and shops and my office on campus, a proximity I had never known in any city. At the travel section, I stared at guidebooks to Los Angeles and to San Francisco, reflecting that such a popular tourist and immigrant destination was what I called home. But then it struck me, which home?

I could not figure out which guide was appropriate because I did not know where I was. I had been struck by dislocasia. I spent a long, long time, perhaps all of twenty seconds, wondering where I stood, utterly fascinated at the blank I drew. Was it that synapses had blown, that I'd fallen off a weird topological fold, that I was dead, or that I had contracted physiological and psychological, spatial and temporal, dislocasia? I was to have numerous bouts with the disease over the next two years, most frequently when I'd wake up, like when I returned to Berkeley and moved into the house of men-without-their-children: the Puerto Rican with sons, preterit divorced; me, a Chicano with daughters, present progressive divorcing; and the Irishman with one of each, future subjunctive divorce. Occasionally the pre-dawn black transition from sleep to waking, and from pre motion to motion, would find me not recognizing anything. And at other times too, in daylight and in midsentence. Yet I had no panic and managed to find some small ironic pleasure at each occurrence: again? Ah, dislocasia.

Dislocasia's characteristic sense of nonlocatability and of being lost seems to me more profound than merely spatial. True, it manifested itself first and foremost as a break in contiguity, as a break in the sense of place, but it always made me feel as if I were displaced from a time line, as if the reason for the dislocation in space were caused in the first instance by a fall from the flow of one time to another.

maze

One reason I could find some joy in spontaneous displacement is that it is such a break with the normal, for usually I have a very good sense of direction, of space and location. Another reason was its attendant sense of wonder.

I got lost on a walk in Mexico City once and quite enjoyed it. Quite simply, I made a wrong turn exiting a shop and zigzagged away in a wholly other direction than I realized or had intended. It was the summer in the middle of my twenties; two of my daughters had been born. I had gone to teach a course in Chicano literature but ended up studying Nahuátl with Juan Luna Cárdenas, an amazing man. I still recall him by his aphorism, "*cuando el indio encanece, el español ni aparece.*"

I left my wife and girls at our apartment for a walk, heading somewhere toward the aptly named Calle Niño Perdido. I didn't know Mexico City very well, so my excursions were still Hansel and Gretel bread crumb treks, paths I paid careful attention to so that I could retrace my steps back. I still conceived the city as linear paths with clearly ascribed destinations at each end, like the metros there or in Paris. I could not yet intuit DF as a field of inhabited zones crossed by a maze of streets.

I walked casually, absorbing impressions, confident in my orientation and sense of direction. I came to a bakery and wondered how Mexican Mexican bread could differ from Chicano Mexican bread. You see, *pan mexicano* is wonderful thing, and before I learned that it was a legacy of French imperialism (the cinco de mayo, Júarez, Maximilian, the French army), that it was an imitation of French pastry, I had long been fascinated by the distinct names, shapes, and textures of the individual pieces in the *panaderías* of East Los Angeles. So I walked into the bakery and absorbed the magic of bread.

When I exited I turned the wrong way, left or right, I do not recall, and found myself on streets I had never seen. That I was lost fascinated me: it was truly serendipitous and the surprise delighted me. And I truly was lost, for not only did I lose track of my trail of bread crumbs, but I was unable to conceive a larger picture of where I might be. I had lost my sense of line, and my sense of field was nonexistent.

When I first lived in London, I got around most often by tube rather than by walking or taking the bus. As a result I got to know the city very well, but for the longest time only according to the sense afforded by the tube lines. When I switched to walking I was able to reconceive the city as a plane and as a field upon which I could envision other spatial relationships. It was as if my sense of the city expanded from the subterranean line to the surface plane, from lines with destination points to a grid of possibilities. For a bit in Mexico City, however, I seemed to exist only as a single point, amazed.

31

maze

 **flight**

While it is not true, I don't lie when I say that the reason I could not live in Ireland is because it is a land without hummingbirds. To think that I would live my days with the absolute impossibility of a chance sighting of one is, after all, a theoretical possibility. They are such magic and such joy I think in part because of how they fly: I think they must be to other birds what birds are to us. When I tried to describe them to Emer and explain why was her island so sad, I could only offer the fact that they could fly backward. It was as inadequate as it was inane, not my best expression as a poet.

I took off for Mexico to expunge a black hole I had placed in my soul while I was living in Westwood, in the days of dislocasia. I drove to Rosarito, Baja California, just beyond Tijuana. I like the border: it seems home to me, between the realities of Mexico and the US, a simulacrum perhaps, the way LA seems compared to Westwood, New York, London. Rosarito is a beach town, between Tijuana and Ensenada, less significantly a tourist destination than either.

I found a hotel on the broad beach at the end of a dirt road. I was the only guest. It was winter a few weeks after the big one in LA; the aftershocks were frequent, if irregular, shaking up things even this far south. The angry earth, the gray sky, and the solitary accommodation all increased the sadness of my spirit, or rather, if I were truly the center of the universe, as I sometimes suspect, earth, sky, and accommodation were sad and gray reflections of my spirit. I'd driven south because I felt like shit and wanted Mexico to fix me. It did.

I walked across the broad beach to the ocean's edge. Everything was gray with only the most muted trace of color. The water was gray, only slightly green; the sand was gray, distantly beige; the sky was gray and gray; I could find no trace of blue in it. There was a strong offshore blowing, and were it not invisible, I would have seen it blow gray against my black heart.

I stood at the edge of the water, turned my back on the sea, and looked back across the sand, face to the wind. The sand, I noticed, was not a single shade, but darker and lighter: blacker, heavy wet sand at my feet and whiter, airy light sand that never got wet in the distance. And in between the extremes there was a continuous spectrum of shade and moisture.

34

flight

Birds must look at hummingbirds with wonder or with incomprehension at the least. I react to the ability to fly the way I imagine birds must to the ability to hover by the tiniest of their genus. No other bird can fly like the hummingbird; the others must wonder what it is like. In my dreams as a child and in my daydreams after, I wonder at the ability.

The strong offshore picked up the dry sand and blew it out to sea. At the water's edge, I could see the bright white sand blow toward me, over the darker and wetter sand and then by me, out to the sea beyond. In what must be a natural trompe l'oeil, the whiter sand seemed to blow especially for me in a widening swath. The wind was stiff: I extended my arms as if wings. The lighter sand blowing over the darker, the noise of wave and wind, the wind itself, and me with wings: for a moment or two I knew what it was to fly. Much later, I related this to my mother; she said that these are moments given by god. An epiphany.

flight

Once I was walking up Bancroft in Berkeley deep in thought when I was enveloped by intense fragrance. It was jasmine. When I turned to the bush, I caught sight of a tiny green hummingbird, darting, hovering, and doing the impossible. It seemed to me a gift, also an epiphany.

10 fall

I was sitting in the Nag's Head pub with Xóchitl, my middle daughter, then nineteen, the same daughter who five years earlier had beaten me up the Pyramid of the Sun at Tenochtitlan when the leading edge of my sole caught stone and humiliated me. I sat proud with my pint, she with her Orange Squash, proud that my daughter had found a great place to stay in London and that she was doing an admirable job at taking care of her life. As her father I marveled at the human irony that this young woman was the same young teenager who left me in defeat on the side of a pyramid and the same little girl who rode her tricycle with the straightest of postures and yet too, the same child who at less than a year of age would respond to my question, *"¿Cuántos años tienes?"* with a loud *"¡Cero!"* She was yet Xóchitl even if different than she had been at any point along the narrative of her life. There in the pub with pride and with a pint or two, it seemed opportune to relinquish patriarchal authority for that narrative's meaning and to listen.

My daughter came back to our table in the corner, drinks in hand, eager to relate what the bartender had told her. Apparently the woman who cleared tables and occasionally brought drinks—it was a large pub—was the bartender's girlfriend and even more apparently, she had been speaking closely with some other guy and had even kissed him. Xóchitl, appearing to the bartender as a random opportunity for feminine exegesis, told him that such an action within his sight meant nothing serious. I, distanced by generation and gender, reserved judgment.

Anyway, as Chaos would have it, the objectionable guy came and sat at the table next to us, as remote a spot as the pub afforded. Out of nowhere the bartender's girlfriend appeared and glided over to his table. Her grace is significant in this retelling because on all other occasions that we'd seen her walk she demonstrated that gait Shakespeare noted of his race four centuries ago: "I grant I never saw a goddess go; / My mistress when she walks treads on the ground."

In the distance, the bartender strained to watch the couple every chance he could. Fortunately, their proximity was such that neither Xóchitl or I could avoid spying. They spoke about little, mostly the fencing of polite social intercourse, but their speech itself was charged with passion. Sadly, it seemed to me, hers more so than his. Yet I remained disinterested, my back to them, and read Xóchitl's silent expressions that marked their significant locutions and gestures.

Enough was enough, however. The bartender came up to the couple in what Xóchitl explained was the most cool of ways: he just said hello. He waited for a response and then made light of the fact that some guy was off in the corner with his girl. Even I noted the labor in that pause, for not only was the woman the sort to be upset by surprise, she stumbled out a vague introduction that said nothing about her relationship with the bartender. The bartender took the hint and left, and so did the other guy, taking flight as soon as the bartender had withdrawn and polite society allows.

Hooked on this compelling story, Xóchitl and I settled in; we got more drinks and crisps, mint and lamb flavor by mistake, I think. The waitress cleaned up every ashtray in the pub, removed every glass and plate and utensil, and retreated to the back room for supplies or to adjust the thermonuclear control. She avoided the bartender like the plague. Since we were uninvolved except for the entertainment factor, it was for us sheer delight. Finally he caught her, but as Chaos would have it, it was across the room, well out of earshot. Fortunately, I sired a daughter for whom distance is no impediment and who gave me a blow-by-blow reading. The bartender gesticulated a bit, angry but calm; the woman looked down, maintaining the posture of guilt. After a while they went about their business, civilized. Show over, my daughter and I took off.

We had walked down Holloway Road to a cash box and after securing a fistful of pounds sterling were walking back in the direction of the pub. As we approached, the woman shot out, delight in face, running in abandon, almost as a child skips. Oblivious, she ran toward us and past, her face full of anticipation, joy even. Xóchitl and I looked to each other, "ah ha," she must be rushing off, covertly, to the other guy.

Then a sharp screech, a thud; we turned, and she lay in the middle of the road. Thinking I had to act, I sent Xóchitl to the pub to call an ambulance; I approached the fallen woman. She lay unconscious, peaceful as if asleep, but in a position like a chalked victim outline. A small silver-gray Japanese car poised just behind her, its windscreen shattered, sunken concave into the passenger compartment, completely fractured but holding still. The driver exited; he was dark, what goes for Paki in London, and extended his cellular phone to me. I waved him off and kneeled beside the still woman. There was no blood, she seemed asleep, dreaming; I put my hand to her shoulder; what else could I do? People gathered, some woman came up and adjusted the woman's skirt; I guess it

fall

had appeared somehow improper. Xóchitl came up and told me that at first she could only find the bartender in the pub and that she could not get herself to tell him his love lay mown down in the street. But she had managed something and help was on the way.

The police chased us off, so we went on with our lives. Late that night, we returned to the pub, and I inquired as to the woman's fate. To my amazement she was sitting at the bar and wearing the same clothes. She was ignorant of my concern, of my interest in a brief dramatic narrative in her life, and that at one point in my life it had seemed the most important thing to touch her, to kneel beside her and lay my hand on her shoulder.

fall

11 prince

When Xóchitl was twelve, St. George's School in Kilburn was invited downtown to participate in an anti-drug campaign. The idea was to stage a "just say no" run around Covent Garden before the media and aristocracy in a tacit expression of solidarity with Nancy Reagan. At the photo-op kicking off the crusade, my daughter and Tani, her African schoolmate, found themselves beside a prince. Foreigners both, they nonetheless stood there representing the abstinent youth of England, beside Edward. Tani extended her hand to shake his; Xóchitl did not, being too cool to do so. He dismissed the girl's gesture, declaring that if he allowed her to touch him, others would wish to do the same. I am proud to say that my daughter found that risible and found him to be such the dork.

So what translates in touch? I ask this not merely of the translation of different social forms of touch, in the matter of styles, but also of the physical link established by the touch. In one way, touching a prince, as well as touching a fallen English woman, is a matter of power. In England, unlike in India, being untouchable confers authority. To deny touch there is to exercise royal power. And yet on, or rather by, quite another hand, the stranger beside Ophelia in the pool of her own blood on Earl's Court Road conferred power. His touch said, "you do not need to get up, or panic, or struggle in the least: I'll be your strength."

And in regard to touch and knowledge: what better way to recognize the anachronistic decadence of a social system that confers power by gene than to listen to the laughter of a twelve-year-old Chicana?

prince

# 12 cartas

At about the same time as the Edward-the-untouchable incident, I took a brief trip from London to Paris to Barcelona to Paris to London. It was all by surface and all in rapid succession. I visited a friend in Paris, lectured on Bakhtin in Barcelona, and then caught a lecture by Derrida on the rue d'Ulm on the way home. Travel by ferry or train is usually at such a pace that my sense of locasia has ample opportunity to adjust to each place. With air travel, however, the ready transition to place is not so much a function of the duration of flight, which is, after all, so brief, as it is that of the shock of airports, something akin to an alarm clock in a most perfect sleep: sharp, absolute, unforgiving.

Translation is most difficult, perhaps, with poetry and jokes. This is so, I believe, because both poem and joke are intricate plays of language, one aesthetic, the other humorous. Translation has been conceived tediously as an arrow shot from one language to the other, so that a Spanish arrow shot to an English target lands as "my aunt's feather is on the table," a bull's eye but alas, no joke. What is wrong with that metaphor is its disconnection, or rather, its connection by flight path alone, so that the context is severed from the content and the result hits or misses apart in the target language. Poets, joke tellers, and Chicanos keep track of language play by course so that metaphors other than spent arrows configure poem, joke, and border articulation.

My three-city, three-national-language tour brought to bear unexpected stress on my sense of linguistic play and translation. If I conceived translation both as an active interplay and as a conflictive spill between different languages, as in the humor, for example, that could so make funny the claim of an embarrassed man in English that he is pregnant in Spanish, then I promulgated a model that could so easily spin out of control when subjected to rapid movement from England, France, and Spain, as it did. Because I am a Chicano poet who enjoys a good joke as well as a solid translation, I take delight in linguistic play and in linguistic interplay, in irony, ambiguity, parody, and dialogism, that is, in the push of the banal to poetry, to humor, or of humanity to the border. Such work is difficult enough in one language, very difficult in translation to a second, and exponentially more so, interactively among three.

My history is such that when I had gone to France

46

cartas

or Spain it was most often from an English-speaking country. So the confluence of language was either English and French or English and Spanish. At least this was the case in Europe. In the Americas, the situation was more complex because I was born and raised in the borderlands where English and Spanish are mixed on both sides of an international frontier. In LA, for example, I took part in the play between, and in between, English and Spanish and Chicano hybrid speech. But away from this element, movement between languages in Europe meant that my focus was not so much on interplay as it was on practical translation, not on the play between but on the arrow from bow to target.

cartas

On the last leg of that three-city tour, I was preparing to return to England when I stopped at a post office in the cinquième. Having had switched already from English to French, then French to Spanish, and then from Spanish to French all caught up with me there at the post office window. I lost myself in translation, awash in a stream of detached signifiers: *letter lettre letra carte-lettre carta post card carte postale postal tarjeta.* Unfortunately for the people in line behind me, I seized that opportunity to delight in the nonsensical dance of words and could communicate nothing intelligible to the counter person.

I dislike Eco's character Salvatore in *The Name of the Rose,* not because his hybrid language connotes heresy, but because the mixing of tongues denotes a mental deficiency for which he is burned at the stake. We live in times, after all, when Rita Patino Quintero can be confined to the Larned State Hospital for twelve years simply because hybrid speech is taken as sign of schizophrenia. At any rate, there at that moment in the French post office, I came to realize something about the play among words that I had undervalued at home in California, Alta as well as Baja. For not only the dynamics of play, but the spin on the inflection, the vantage point of the speaker, or perhaps more correctly, the site from which the speaker comes, participates in the meaning of the play. Place of origin could act to define the line of play in language as much as it does the trajectory of wind. Broken, confused, or lost, that trace of origin could lead to a heretic's death, a Chicana's incarceration, or a confused wait in line.

cartas

13 the dead

I spent my last teenage year among the dead, avoiding their bodies, afraid, and absolutely convinced that communication with them is impossible. The dead are not human, the corpse has the stillness of a photograph, the presence of stone. The dying human looks absolutely alive till death, then the body, absolutely dead.

To avoid Vietnam I went to college, and to pay for college I worked my sophomore year at the LA County Coroner's Office. It seemed ironic, during the times of a most ironic war, that my flight from killing abroad was to work as a custodian for the dead at home. I was a stock boy, which meant that I moved paper before it was written on and signed and thereby rendered official. The paper trail would take me by necessity, pushing my little cart, through the morgue, the place full of dead bodies, between my office and the storage room in the basement.

On the first day of work I confessed my fear of corpses to fellow student worker Chas T. He led me with our cart of forms through the morgue and told me to avert my eyes until he said we were clear. When he did we were beside a corpse, my first and a sight I recall to this day: the body of a tall woman, stiff as wood, and the color of Caucasian flesh transformed to a purple mahogany thing. I was as angry with him as I was shocked, all of which provided a sound beginning for friendship.

The Coroner's office seemed to me a hell for the detritus of humanity, the used up, discarded flesh that had been the indigent unable to die in a doctor's care, the assassinated presidential candidate, or the overdosed sex icon. We custodians too seemed similar, albeit living, detritus. The nonprofessional workers, those of us without degrees, were all minorities, mostly African-American. The doctors and technicians seemed to be either immigrants unable to practice in the US or Anglo-Americans, the sort of doctors from film noir, quirky and with secret pasts. The Coroner, who stayed in his office and whom I never saw except when he sent me to Philippe's for a lamb dip sandwich, was Japanese and regularly had it out with county higher-ups and the press.

Chas and I were left alone to regulate the flow of paper, left alone in accordance with the spirit of the place, which was a spirit of low-level compassion for fellow living humans. Unlike the dead, we shared a common vitality. We related to one another much the way Aussies and Kiwis do in England, or Anglo-Canadians and Anglo-Americans do in a Slavic country. Chas and I would deliberately run low on some form or volunteer to secure a crate of gloves, so that we could take a county car and spend the day on the road. We would alternate such excursions at optimal frequency so as not to be denied the privilege. Our access to the car, freedom from the workplace, and attempts at cavalier attitudes made us the self-proclaimed gifts to the young female clerical staff. Young, because the older Black women dismissed us as boys.

We each had our favorite excursions as well as those we undertook simply because we were paid to do so. I had two favorites: one with Jill, to El Tepeyac, and the other with Bonnie to the USC medical center at LA County General. Manuel's El Tepeyac is a prime Mexican restaurant in East Los, situated ironically beside the Evergreen Cemetery and close enough to downtown to fill with suits at lunch. To this day I take delight in upsetting the bourgeoisie, but Jill was restless and easily bothered by the righteous, those aghast that her black body was not seated across another equally so. Bonnie, the only young

the dead

and Anglo woman among the secretaries, was from Greeley, Colorado, on an urban hiatus of sorts. She'd wait in the car while I'd rushed into the hospital for a box of rubber gloves, then we'd park somewhere high in Lincoln Heights, overlooking a freeway, and talk and laugh. On other occasions, I would acquiesce to drive to the printer's, a most boring trip, a short drive that required a long wait, far too long to bring anyone along and too boring to laugh.

the dead

14  signs

Throughout that time among dead, I believed that talk with the body was not possible even though touch was. The Hall of Justice is a shady gray cube of a building, a solid testimony to order overlooking the Santa Ana Freeway. It is the house of justice for social detritus: there are cells for felons, courts for their judgment and sentencing, sheriff's deputies to marshal restraint, and on the ground level, if you entered from Spring Street, it was the work place for the custodians of the dead. From Broadway, the Coroner's was one-level subterranean.

I avoided the portentous entrance down from Broadway, preferring instead the portal on Spring, flush with the surface as it was and suggesting life and a season of creation. By my last days there, the end of the summer I'd leave LA, my struggles to remain on the level with life in the house of the dead had been marked, over and again, by signs of the dead.

Like for example the sign of the X, not of the cross, but of the letter, as in X marks the spot. They were three, girls my age, hanging around at the Spring

Street entrance. Chas took no interest in white hippie chicks, but Lewis, the Jewish artist from Berkeley, did, so he and I would take our breaks, and he his lunch times as well, with them. The three girls milled, killing time, waiting outside in the daylight for the verdict of the big trial going on within. We liked them, but I lost interest when they shaved their heads and carved Xs in their foreheads. Lewis on the other hand had fallen in love and had been invited to the Spahn ranch: what did I think, should he go? To this day, I would find romance difficult with the devotee of a murderer or at the site of ritual killing.

But how could Lewis not be confused there in the light of day? He had, after all, the most claustrophobic of jobs at the Coroner's, toiling away all summer in the back of a vault beneath the morgue. His place was marked off from the rest of the office as the final repository for the last detritus of the long dead. For after the body had undergone autopsy and had been sent off for funeral, and even after the still remains that had housed the human spirit had long since decayed, Lewis managed the care of its ultimate piece. His job consisted of opening jars that had exceeded their five-year shelf life, emptying their contents into special bags and throwing the jars into other special bags. The contents of the jars were small bits of the dead: an embryo, a gall stone, and various other well catalogued but unrecognizable fragments that had once been vital. The Coroner's care of the dead continued well beyond the autopsy; words were stored on paper and body bits in jars. Above at ground level, I ensured the supply of blank forms; below in the basement, Lewis disposed of the last physical trace.

To visit Lewis at work I would pass through the morgue and do my best to avoid perceiving by any of my five senses an infant on the floor scale, a mahogany body, or a mass of decomposition that had been human a couple of weeks before being locked up in the trunk of a car. Down in the underground without windows and amid tunnels lay Lewis's dark cell. It hid beside the overflow room, which was actually a room-sized refrigerator for those times of natural or unnatural mass death, and the Sheriff's vault for confiscated drugs. You could smell the marijuana, thick, emanating from behind the heavy door, but no custodian of the dead had access to that space. What was accessible, however, was the storage room for the unclaimed effects of the dead: a room of brown envelopes, each containing what had been in the possession of humans at the moment of death. And of course, many of them did die holding onto drugs. Lewis would tear into envelope after envelope and take marijuana joints, pills, lots of pills, and whatever else smacked of contraband. We would retire to the far reaches of his cell to talk. He'd ingest whatever he found, and we'd watch the occasional deputy cross by the door.

By the end of that summer, I had borne witness to many signs of the dead, which had, for no clear reason, entwined words with bits of flesh. When Oscar

Zeta Acosta came through, one of the Black secretaries pointed out "the Chicano lawyer" to me, so that I could see one of my own, the only one, who entered the place with any authority. Zeta had come to confront the authorities in a routine matter, the death of a Chicano in police custody. In *Revolt of the Cockroach People*, Zeta describes that visit to the Coroner's and how he gathered evidence by directing the severing of bits of flesh from the body of Robert Fernández. Zeta ends the novel recalling the police killings of Fernández and of Rubén Salazar.

My job ended when I came into work where Salazar's body had been brought in, after having been there when he was killed. I had been there when an LA County Sheriff deputy killed Rubén Salazar, there in a general, yet most profound. sense, for I did not find out till later how the tear gas projectile that had been designed to pierce walls had ripped through his life in the Silver Dollar Cafe on Whittier Boulevard. I was there somewhere down the street, being chased by police who were shooting tear gas canisters from the ground and dropping them from helicopters. Salazar and I were both there as journalists: he was the most eminent voice for Chicanos, a journalist for the *LA Times* and KMEX television; I was freelancing for the *LA Free Press*. But I survived, and he did not. Afterward I ensured that there was paper for my boss to record the cause of death, a "projectile wound of the left temple area causing massive injury to the brain."

15 gun

So when the police had my daughter in an assassination position, kneeling, gun to her head, I took care to choose and phrase my words precisely. I pulled into the driveway when Junior, son of the deaf couple next door, ran up to me saying the police had Marisol at the end of the block. I wonder about Junior's self-articulation, being as he was mixed, half Chicano, but raised completely without the sounds of parental words in any language.

There were two policemen, a man and a woman, Anglos both; the man had the pistol at my daughter's head. My wife came up to me as I reached the scene. Both policemen watched us speak, watched the brief exchange by what was taken for an irrational Mexican mama and whatever I was to prove to be.

I never did write the article about the police riot and the destruction on Whittier Boulevard that culminated in the deaths of Gilberto Díaz, Lyn Ward, and Rubén Salazar. *The LA Free Press,* radical journal that it was, had had plenty of eyewitness and analysis, so in the face of such quantity there was no need for my piece. A week before it did run a piece of mine that described an upcoming demonstration, what was to become the largest Chicano protest against the war. But the description of the event itself, of the chaos and the killing, I did not write because of a loss of faith. You see, the news reports, especially those on television, lied, not merely slanted in bias, but outright lied about wild Chicano radicals and innocent peace officers. I lost faith in truth, in the hard link between word and event.

So I extended what police want: absolute acquiescence: it was a small price for my daughter's brain left intact. I addressed the pig in my very best rational liberal humanist, Protestant work ethic individualist, law-abiding and God-fearing all-American speech. I put to the test the PhD and years of watching television. I did my best to speak my daughter out of insignificance and to move her image in his mind to an equivalency with that of a suburban Anglo girl of the bourgeoisie, the national icon he would be loathe to kill.

In the end I spoke well but did nothing. I think that had I not lost faith as a young man in East Los Angeles, I might have lost a daughter that day in San José.

16 faith

I spent the first years of my life in East Los Angeles and my school years down the boulevard, farther east in Whittier. In between those two homes, I spent the fourth year of my life in Montebello, just off Beverly Boulevard. From that time and space, an interstice in my personal narrative, I recall two blood incidents, very small incidents, but ones that did foster a particular faith that I was to lose much later.

The first incident is as brief as it is vague: my sister threw a toy rifle at me, hitting me on the ear; I remember almost nothing else but bleeding and a texture of wound. The second is a more developed story, reflecting, I think, its greater significance in the narrative of my life. María Luísa, or Tata, as she was called, used to bite me. She did this often and with neither mercy nor provocation. She'd bite into my arm, for example, and no matter what I'd do, she would not let go until she so pleased. In truth, my protestations were weak; they were verbal except for the physical attempts to break free. I took very seriously my mother's prohibition against hitting girls. As a result, I was repeatedly punctured and indented and made to cry. Finally, in a scene I recall reminiscent of a Bruce Lee film, my mother relented and authorized, no, rather demanded the use of violence. The next time Tata bit me, I pushed her off and chased her. I picked up a shard of glass and cut her back as she ran away screaming.

There is a lesson in violence, and it is called upon to justify its use: violence can put an end to some action. As much as I would like to decry this with a rebuttal like violence only exacerbates, or something of the sort, I don't because, in truth, Tata never bit me again, Rubén Salazar never wrote again and, in illustration of its absence, a daughter of mine persists to this day because violence was not employed.

faith

17 fear

Fear, unlike violence, is a slow burn. While a gunshot, cut, or rape happens with brilliant intensity, it is bounded by its absence. Fear, on the other hand, is a long story with a long blur of suffering and the longing for release. For this reason it seems often spatial, an emotion attached to a location: a bedroom, the ghetto, hell. And it is also for this reason rendered temporal: a fear of old age, night, the moment before going on stage. Its extension across space and time, as well as the familiar delineation of fear in story lines, give the emotion a particular palpability. We assign meaning to its presence, dimension, and direction when we attach fear to place, time, to thing. Our sense of fear is its link, the connection we sense between the irrational and its object.

Twice in poems I took up the matter of fear. That both were long poems, prosey, and of similar tone seems to me to indicate that I find such form appropriate for such content. I wrote *"À mon seul désir"* in two voices, one lyric, the other prosaic, one masculine, the other feminine, yet all in Spanish except for its French title. The title serves for me as the link, necessary for an evocation of the emotion, with a particular place, time, and object. It is a poem as much about fear as it is about a life, as much about an irrational undercurrent as it is about a real walk.

fear

It was winter in Paris, early February; the streets were wet, the air, cool, heavy. Two of us had time to kill, so Dominique decided to show me a bit of her city. The night before, there had been a disagreement among friends: three women and an Australian emigrant argued the oldest church in Paris. I watched them go at it, silently, lacking as I was in local knowledge, but hoping that St-Julien-le-Pauvre beat out St-Germain-de-Prés because I so liked the poor name. And as it turned out, my walk with Dominique did take me to very old religious sites, yet the matter in contention remained unresolved.

We walked by the Tour St-Jacques, the odd ruins of a church, a solitary corner, standing as if it had been meant to be a tower. We wandered into the end of an evening mass. And we went to the Musée de Cluny, the site of old Roman baths and a museum of medieval art. It is there that a most famous set of Lady and Unicorn tapestries hangs. The tapestries are of a piece, six hangings, one to each of the senses and a sixth, *"À mon seul désir..."* Their story, I imagine, is a rejection of the worldly in favor of the divine, played out in the rejection of the perceptible, one sense at a time. The ultimate object of desire is unclear, however, because the title piece, "to my one desire...," is not completely legible: a final letter remains indecipherable as if a vague initial of the absent object of desire.

By the time we stood before the tapestry, Dominique and I had spent enough time walking together, sharing sights, and absorbing the signs of French Catholicism that it was easy to turn the focus to ourselves. I was very much taken by the tapestry's flat perspective that surrounded the yellow-haired Lady with fantastic animals on a single plane. I pointed out a strange representation of a bird, and Dominique confided her fear of birds, a fear such that she would not eat them. It was not a profound fear; it was a casual one, casual yet real. Its object struck me as comical, impossible as such, of course, because it was not a fear specifically my own.

fear

Dominique resembles the Lady in the *"À mon seul désir..."* tapestry, blonde, pale, and thin, similar but without the unicorn and in twentieth-century dress with green eyelashes. And why not? The story of a denial of the senses and an embracing of an elusive desire is woven into the fabric of her race, as much as it is woven into her individual story: in presence and dimension and object of fear. And I am touched by that emotion when I recall the ambient elements of color, moisture, fabric, and a present but unintelligible object of emotion.

# 18 being

The subject of expression, both in subject as agent and as in subject matter, works and works out differently in lines of lyric and in lines of story. Given a like object in the writing of poetry and prose, the realization of desire, for example, the fact of method of each yields disparate results. Take for example the issue of ontology.

A common story of the becoming of a writer of narrative is one of living a life in narration. Accomplished fiction writers from George Orwell to Sandra Cisneros have explained a curious phenomenon in their youth. It seems their future call was evidenced in a self-conscious narration of their banal acts. That is, as they undertook some action, walking up stairs, for example, they narrated their actions to themselves silently as if reading description in a novel. An odd and, in truth, somewhat tedious undertaking to my mind, which I'm sure so occurs to me because god did not make me to write fiction.

That fiction writers would look back upon life as if it were a narrative sequence of events that lead causally to their present makes sense because they are fiction writers. Notwithstanding my employment of tautology, it is in character for fiction writers to both conceive and depict the human being as a line of unfolding causes and effects. That their formation should be described in a personal narration is appropriate and demonstrates a fundamental faith in an essential fabric of writing and being. I think that the world must make sense for them as an ontology of sequence, that one becomes in order.

So if in life the fiction writer reaches for a door and narrates the sequence of events as they occur, what does the poet do? To answer that the poet reaches for the door and thinks *more* or *Othello* may point to something. But to merely insert a poetic break in a sequence of narrative logic is an attempt to figure the poetic in the line of the prosaic. Something of the opposite happens when one seeks to define metonymy by synonym, that is, seeks metaphors for metonymy. But then if we subtract narration, what are we left in the conception and description by the poet? Perhaps we are left with an emphasis on image rather than story. If the object of desire is left illegible in *"À mon seul désir…,"* what is the domain of that object? Are those French words poetry? fiction?

During my first winter after leaving Los Angeles, I found myself in Santa Cruz attending a reading by

Galway Kinnell. He read his bear poems, masculine verse about hunting and killing and surviving in nature. After reading one poem, he explained in casual commentary how he had invented the method of killing the bear, that of freezing a bone curved in meat so that it would thaw, uncurl, and rip the insides of the bear that ate it. Clever, I thought, but somewhere there seemed to be a lie. In the middle of his reading it began to snow: I could see white flakes against the dark redwoods outside. I had just left LA and had never seen snow fall from the sky. I pondered: should I finish the reading or see the snow. I went outside and caught flakes in my hands my hair and my life for the first time.

being

19 race

Let me digress here. I have remained interested in a line of thought, whether it manifest as a progression toward the absent object of desire, as a connection to the fragmentary and dead, or as a structure for an emotive logic. Meaning, it seems, given dimension, direction, and impetus, accrues. Yet besides considering linear movement from point A to point B and on to C, one can well ask, literally, how fast?

In auto racing there is a virtual line on the race track, an optimum path to realize maximum speed. But that is not quite correct, for the line is taken to yield the least elapsed time. Yet inasmuch as the consideration of distance over time can be expressed as the ratio *speed,* less time means greater speed. But the fact remains that the race is won by the one who crossed the finish line first, in the least time, regardless of any speed along the way. A line is therefore driven that permits the circumvention of the track with the expenditure of the fewest fractions of seconds.

Tracks for road racing combine straights and turns and changes in elevation and slant. The course of a lap can include straights of varying lengths; turns, left and right; curves of various arcs, with decreasing or increasing radii; elevation changes in the length of the course and slope changes across its width: a menagerie of the chicane, esses, hairpin, carousel, and off-camber. But for all its variation, the road course is a single surface, turning, rising, falling, but never leaving the track plane. The race car's line is flat on the pavement; it is not like the line of the airplane or the swimmer underwater. And across that flat track plane, the racer works out the shortest time line.

That line does mark a time sense for the circuit: it defines the track from edge to edge with the sole purpose to cut time. Toward that end, the driver can do little to control distance, a lap after all being a lap, and so is left with the only other variable in the equation: speed. And so to diminish time and the duration of the race, the driver rationally follows a line of maximum speed. In general, the rule of the line is that most time is cut on the straights, and so it is essential to take them at maximum speed. Corners become slingshots from which cars are thrown onto straights, and so the racing line becomes the path of the fastest exiting speed from the corners leading to straights.

Because of this, driving a race is something quite

different from driving the streets. On rigorous road courses at maximum speed there is little of the sense of casual motoring. First, there is the matter of commitment to the line. At maximum speed the car is at the very edge of control; the balance of a car in a high speed corner can easily be lost by simply changing lines or applying the brakes. Each lap is a set sequence of optimum shifting, braking and cornering points with little rational opportunity for variety. Second, there is the matter of constraint. The driver, especially in formula cars, is tightly wedged into the race car. The driver must shoe horn deep in the cockpit and cannot see his knees, let alone his feet. He can only see behind and to the side by the use of the two tiny side mirrors. He is held pressed into the seat by a six-pointed star of belts, and his entire body, except for the eyes, is covered in flame-retardant material. Blood type must be displayed on the suit.

race

I didn't race much because of the cost and eventually sold the car for the down payment on a house. Yet one residual benefit to this day from racing is the particular bond I formed with my youngest daughter. When I worked on the car, endless hours taking it apart completely, Mireya would often accompany me. She was in diapers and would stand on the seat, grip the small steering wheel, and listen to me describe camber, sway, or the appropriate Hewland ratios. I thought she was fascinated by the stuff and that

I was imparting carbon monoxide receptivity and a
love for the sport. It wasn't until I next got to Willow
Springs that I found out her interest was not in racing
and not even in the car, but rather in the steering
wheel itself. Its leather cover had proved irresistible
for my teething offspring, and she had gnawed her
way through.

Turn nine at Riverside was a long, sweeping right
hander at the end of a long straight just before the
esses. This meant it was a fast turn: you entered it at
top speed, very little scrubbed off, and you shot out
barely able to ride out the quick left, right, left. The
turn itself was broad and banked, giving the illusion
that you could motor casually across its width. But at
the end of the straight, you entered it as fast as your
car could go; that straight, after all, was where you
most ate the clock. The corner was rimmed by a low
concrete wall, which seemed to race with you through
the turn as you held tight to the line. It was the wall's
absolutely unforgiving concrete that awaited those
who strayed off line and that had grown men scream
in their helmets there lap after lap.

I pushed the blue formula car onto the straight
after badly negotiating an off-camber left-hander: I
never seemed to get set up right for the long straight.
But I'd get on the straight and go, up the gears, right
foot to the floor. I'd pass and be passed on that
straight and then fall into turn nine. I'd push the car

till the rear wheels were about to break loose and hold on. In my peripheral vision, I'd watch the wall running beside me, marking the absolute edge of my track. In the low, single-seat car, I sat, or rather reclined, so my eye level was less that three feet above the pavement. The wall was a bit taller. As I approached the end of the turn, I knew my line would take me from the inside right to the outside left edge when I exited, that is, toward the wall. At the exit, everything would speed up. The fast turn seemed calm till its end, then, in a rush across the track to the exit of the turn, it looked as if the wall came rushing up to me. Every time I exited that turn, lap after lap, I'd watch that wall, and every time, I came close, inches at most, from hitting the edge of the wall, and yet every time, I shot out beyond, off into the esses.

race

20

auto body

While the car may be an instrument for linear motion on the road course of a single plane, meaning can be ascribed by a recourse to other levels, higher and lower. This after all is a trick of humanity: any act undertaken or object envisioned can be considered from remove. The real and down-to-earth movement from green flag to checkered, or from one neighborhood to another in the city, can come to mean life. For if memory divided by place is the ratio of experience, it is precisely by undertaking the drive that we arrive at meaning. And the more intense the experience, the more meaningful our life story.

The other plane from which we reflect upon our linear motion can be, at times, the very fabric of life itself. Consider two drives, one in the high desert north of LA, the other in the city.

I particularly like the track at Willow Springs because of its terrain. It is at the base of a hill in a wide expanse of desert. The track wanders up and down and around without the need for crash walls: if you spun out on the hill side, gravity would prevent you from going far; if you did on the plain side, the very worst would be a long walk back through tumbleweed. The desert offered a measure of security, for upon losing control and falling away from the racing line, drivers would confront nothing but absent expanse.

auto body

One weekend, for diversion, they ran the races in the opposite direction. This effectively created a new track: the traditional line was useless, and I had to spend the practice sessions trying to plot a new one. The race came all too soon, and I found myself with just the most sketchy idea of a line. I did not have the comfort of clarity, the sure knowledge of well-defined breaking points and corner apexes. Going the other way, the history of the course was annulled; even the streaks of black rubber across the corners meant nothing.

At one point, I decided on a strategy based on a weak logic. I put faith in an algebraic or empirical sense of equivalency: Formula Ford equaled Formula Ford, therefore I could take the same line at the same speed and experience the same results as any other. I tucked the blue Winklemann FF in line behind a black Merlin FF at the end of the straight and followed it into the broad left-hander that had been, in the track's former incarnation, the sweeping right-hander that lead to the long straight. The black car delayed braking longer than I would have and took a turning point farther into the turn as well. I followed and lost it.

As I turned into the turn, the rear wheels broke loose, sending the tail of the car out sideways as if in race with the front. I corrected, but it was too late. About crashing in formula cars, there are several points. First, it is rare to go airborne. Unless you ride over the wheels of another car, the chances are you will spin round and round until some law of physics makes you stop. Second, speed is not the issue. The cars do not have speedometers, and performance is measured by a legion of timekeepers to the ten thousandth of a second. And besides, during the spin the control the driver exercises over direction and rate is completely gone. And third, race cars are hard to start, so once you are spinning out of control the best you can do is to hold on, put in the clutch, and give it some gas so as not to kill, at least, the motor.

So I did just that, gripped the then useless-for-steering wheel, and tried to keep the motor alive. I also closed my eyes. I could see no use for vision at the time. Eventually after a most spectacular spin, which began, incidentally, at well over a hundred miles per hour, I came to a stop in a great cloud of dust. There was dirt in my eyes and inside the balaclava, in my mouth and thick in the air so that I had no idea where I was. Was I outside the track, halfway to Las Vegas;

auto body

inside the track; or was I, horror, still on the track? And the motor was dead. Would a car or two or more come shooting in the cloud and smash into me? Crashing was not a main fear of mine, but fire, being trapped in a burning car, was. I thanked god that the gas tank between the motor and me, maybe three inches behind me, held only five gallons. I wore a suit that would retard burning for fifteen seconds, so what was five gallons?

Then I got hit on the helmet two times: it was a corner worker, fire extinguisher in hand. I could see him standing beside me; the dust cleared. I was in the dirt, inside, and more importantly, off, the track. He motioned, was I OK? I hit the starter button and sur-prise, the motor came to life. I put it in first, and spun great plumes of dirt and got back into the fray.

It was an epiphany of sorts, for I knew then that I was immortal. Or perhaps not quite, but I knew that death would not take me unless I relented at least partially.

A few years earlier in Los Angeles I drove a VW bug on a short drive from City Terrace to Lincoln Heights, neighborhoods that straddle the San Bernardino Freeway. I was in the offices of La Raza Unida, the political party and the radical journal, when a call came in from the offices of Los Tres del Barrio: bring cameras; the police were about to begin shooting. There were only three of us in the office; it was late. And because we were young, none of us veteranos of the movement, we said we'd go and did.

The drive is short, literally just across the freeway, but at that time the distance from Raza Unida to Los Tres was measured in ideological miles. The three of us jumped into my sister's beige VW with the intention to bear witness. We were political activists and believed literally in a *raza unida*. Whoever called us probably had been the same: naive, enthusiastic, and not yet embittered by real-world politics. Actually, it hadn't been that long since both organizations struggled together, but at that later moment our drive was more like one between antagonistic Chicano neighborhoods, which it was, from Varrio Geraghty Lomas to Hazard. Yet while the three of us clearly identified as Raza Unida and did our political work in Lomas, we saw no reason not to go.

We got there in a matter of minutes, the last glow of daylight quickly vanishing. None of us had ever been to the offices of Los Tres; we felt like war correspondents going to bear witness for the raza. We found the office at the base of a slope, across the street from an open space of grass and palm trees. A crowd had gathered out front, perhaps sixty or so of all ages, clearly not just the college radicals, but the neighborhood folk as well. I drove the VW with great caution, for as we neared we saw the police vehicles and, one by one, marksmen in riot gear became visible

auto body

behind the trees. Police raids of Chicano offices, those of La Raza Unida or the Brown Berets, for example, were common fact. And Los Tres seemed to warrant a special attention because it existed to defend three Chicanos, Alberto Ortiz, Juan Fernández and Rudy Sánchez, imprisoned for shooting and paralyzing an undercover narcotics officer, Bobby Canales.

auto body

The drive itself seemed unreal, like a drive in fog I once took in Santa Cruz, which inspired a poem that took twenty years to complete. It seemed to pass silently, very, very slowly, as if we were still and it was the world that gyrated almost imperceptibly outside. We passed the marksmen and let them see our faces, the license plate, and did what you are supposed to do before killers: look them in the eyes and promise to remember. For whatever reason the operation was called off, and the police retreated for another day. We had not stopped nor had needed to; we bore witness to life from the confines of a car driving in circles.

 **maze**

There was a time, over the matter of a few days, that I traveled to Northern Italy and to Northern Ireland in the hospitality of women amid terrorists. I was living in Sligo at the time, so the journey to Italy was by air through London after a drive to Dublin. The journey from Sligo to Northern Ireland was simpler, an easy drive three hours east. I visited the graves of the tragically dead, Juliet Capulet in Italy and Bobby Sands in Northern Ireland, and in Belfast I was attacked by a tree.

I went to Italy to read poetry in Milan and in Treviso, which is just inland from Venice. It was at the time of the Biennalle, the big European arts festival that is held in Venice, as the name implies, biannually. The reading in Milan was a tiny affair at a bookstore not far from the galleria. The reading in Treviso was well attended, the last in the series, *rosso de sera*.

I read in English and in Spanish with an Italian translator at my side. Except for the requisite lag, being translated at the moment proved a delightful yet curious phenomenon. I'd read then pause. The audience would look to Elena for the Italian version of the English but would tend to stay focused on me through the Spanish. After the readings in both cities there was a period for questions, a feature not often the case in the readings I've done before English-speaking audiences in the US or Ireland. The period of questions and answers seemed to make for an air of greater intimacy because of the presence of the translator: she was our living icon, testifying to our characteristically human struggle to understand and be understood.

All of which was particularly interesting in Italy. My poems are interlingual poems, mostly English or Spanish or English and Spanish, but some decidedly more complex. In short, they are border poems, playing in the linguistic terrain characteristic of the zones of international frontiers. So translation of a sort is a dynamic central to my verse. And inasmuch as my poems delight in a give and take across languages, both in form and in content, they seemed to hold themselves up to the Italians as self-articulating artifacts, self-consciously inviting participation. Be that as it may, it was more the Italian audience than the poems themselves that shaped the course of the reading: they had read selections from *Cantos* in translation and were poised to interrogate and criticize. My work had appeared in Italian in a literary journal devoted to the politics of poetry. Baldus takes its name from an early modern macaronic poet who combined Latin and the vernacular, and so in a sense, my work found a welcome home there. There was a sense of intimacy, one that centered around the desire to come to grips with the impossible task we undertake when we try to understand one another. When I left the Treviso reading and had late dinner with the host poet and his mother, I was told that an epigraph from a poem of mine had been used to mark the entrance to a section of paintings at the Biennalle. That, the interest in my work, and an argument over what Lombards purport to be fresh mozzarella in the north, left me moved and thoroughly taken with the place.

On our drive back to Milan, Elena pulled the red Volkswagen off the highway in Verona to show me the *tomba Giulietta*. I am fascinated by the great manifestations of human spirit in places such as cathedrals and the tombs of fictional characters. Both cathedral and tomb, after all, attest to our humanity and affirm in celebration of the species. In the way that the Sistine chapel can impress the atheist with the sense and passion of faith, and by the way, I find the question of whether or not the nonbeliever comes to believe not interesting, in that way, the real place and the physical effects of fictional characters affect me profoundly. And what it is that so strikes me is the fact of desire.

The tomb of Romeo's beloved lies in the center of a dark room in a renaissance building. The tomb looks like a stone bathtub in the middle of the floor. That I was not the first to make pilgrimage is evident by the bits of paper. In the alcove and the slits for light there are testaments to romance: tiny notes on metro tickets, pages from address books, and torn envelopes, truly not professions of faith, but statements of desire. Most were written in Italian, mostly by women, yet all written in the hand of one in love, one having lost love or not having received love. They declared hearts' desires; they made affirmations before the tomb of the tragically dead lover. On occasion they asked Juliet to intercede. I don't think they are motivated the same way that motivates the pilgrim at Tepeyac, Lourdes, or Mecca, for there really isn't faith at their core. What there is, is desire. And who can say which is stronger, faith or desire? In the dark of a small room in Verona, there is ample testimony to the human power of desire.

maze

In Belfast I took my daughters to Milltown Cemetery to visit the grave of Bobby Sands. There is a poem by Sharon Doubiago that juxtaposes his tragic story, a long withering away, of death by starvation, with the cruel irony of decadent life continuing at the same moment. "Hunger" traces the story of the 217-day series of hunger strikes at Maze prison from March 1 to October 3, 1981, which resulted in 10 deaths: Bobby Sands, dead after 66 days of hunger; Francis

Hughes, 59 days; Raymond McCreesh, 61 days; Patsy O'Hara, 61 days; Joe McDonnell, 61 days; Martin Hurson, 45 days; Kevin Lynch, 71 days; Kiernan Doherty, 73 days; Tom McElwee, 62 days; and Mickie Devine, 69 days. "Hunger" details the starvation of 10 bodies, 10 Irishmen whose desire to live free was realized by the final power left the weak, that to say no even to their own flesh. Against this, the poem juxtaposes the English desire for power and the power of desire in the fairy tale wedding and honeymoon of Princess Diana, which took place in the middle of the death strike.

Bobby Sands died on cinco de mayo 1981 and is buried in the IRA section of Milltown, in a plot for three. A headstone marks the site: VOLUNTEERS / TERENCE O'NEILL / BOBBY SANDS / JOE MCDONNELL. The plot is plainly formal, bordered by a teal railing, adorned by small flowers and ribbons in the tricolor of the republic. That it is so dressed up is somehow fitting, for Bobby's death was the cumulation of protests that began with an incident about dress. In 1976, Ciaran Nugent demanded recognition as a political prisoner and refused to wear a prisoner's uniform. From this sprang the blanket protest at Maze prison: three and a half years wearing only blankets and living in awful conditions. The protesters were confined to bare cells, and in response to having their food thrown in by the guards, they smeared their excrement on the walls. Three and a half years wearing blankets and living in shit. This action cumulated in a hunger strike, from October 27 to December 18, 1980. Only after this and after facing the options available to those with power only over their own bodies, they resolved to strike for recognition or until death. Sands and the other nine starved, while the English and American media delighted in the story of a princess and a prince and the ritual reproduction of a system of gene supremacy that the enlightened parts of the world had cast off long ago.

My friend Camille took us to Milltown and pointed out the names and dates on stone in a long history of resistance. She pointed where Michael Stone came up from the highway with automatic weapon and grenades and attacked a group of mourners, wounding fifty and killing three. She told us of many other deaths, of deaths by mistakes of all sorts. She described the facts of apartheid and took us through housing projects very much like Pico Gardens or Maravilla in East LA: poverty, segregation, police surveillance, and cultural nationalist murals. Camille, Sharon Doubiago, and I all had been raised in Los Angeles, but only Camille had emigrated and made Belfast her home. She and I had gotten to know each other in Berkeley and as she says, emphasizing the irony, despite the bombings and the harassment she gets from British soldiers, she is safer in Belfast than she was in Oakland. Statistically she is correct. What does this say about my life, about my daughters' lives? I had heard Bernadette Devlin once talk about this irony of safety amid terror, life amid death.

At one point my daughters and I found ourselves waiting for Camille to come out of class. We sat on a low brick wall at the entrance to Queen's University, on the aptly named University Road. The day was pleasant if a bit too gray and cool for summer. While waiting, I thought about violence and colonialism and the fortress called a police station that overlooks Belfast's Catholic barrio. I wondered about the university: it must, after all, be the Queen's, not merely in name, but owned personally by Elizabeth, the way Hyde Park and the Falkland Islands are. I was feeling particularly Catholic there at the portal to the Protestant university when all of a sudden out of nowhere I was struck in the face and in the groin. I recoiled in pain but could make absolutely no sense. Then I figured it out: there at my feet lay a thick hunk of royal branch, a small log, I like to think. Apparently, Elizabeth's tree had attacked me, crashing first into my mouth and then my genitals. What did it mean? Was this a natural expression in a country without freedom of speech? Was I being censored so as to neither reproduce textually or sexually?

My two friends in Northern Ireland and Northern Italy have lived close to terrorists. Camille's husband

maze

served prison time for his activities but has given up violence and works instead on cultural change. He teaches Irish language and culture in a center that looks very much like similar Chicano organizations. Elena's boyfriend's brother had served a longer sentence. He remains proud that he neither informed nor recanted, both of which are heavily desired by the Italian police. On the flight from the land of one friend to that of the other, I sat next to a Spanish woman, María, who worked for a Formula One organization in London. My surname, she noted, is Basque, which in Spain signifies ethnic minority and ETA, the nationalist, separatist organization, and terrorism. However we did not speak of terror but rather of desire and poetry.

22 color

Desire in painting must be nothing like desire in poetry. Color too, must be different. I find it hard to imagine desire painted, a depiction of its object perhaps, presented in the color of blood. Desire seems verbal, textual, to me: a novel of lust, a lyric of lack. This might well be because I work in words and envision the world in their terms. And so color in my poems must miss the color spread on canvas the way word and phrase are never pigment but the word and phrase for pigment.

I went to a show of work by Frida Kahlo at the Mexican Museum in San Francisco. Along with retablos and portraits, undoubtedly as the curator's supplement, were words: excerpts from Frida's diary printed huge on the walls beside the paintings. My job as a poet prescribes that I pay attention to words, and I was drawn to those of this painter, but beyond this, I was particularly taken because I so often wonder what of an artist transcends media.

My experience of bearing witness to artists' expression in alternate media has been associated with death. I arrived in Paris days after Julio Cortázar died and thereby forever missed the opportunity to see him play jazz. And when I was twenty, my friend Tad and I made a pilgrimage from Santa Cruz to Kenneth Patchen's house in Palo Alto. He was too near death to receive visitors, but his wife gave us a small stack of postcard-sized reproductions of his poem paintings, or painted poems, whichever they were. And of course by the time I stood in San Francisco before the excerpts from Frida Kahlo's diary, she had long since died.

I grew excited when I realized what Frida's text was. At last I could get insight into the transition across media from color to word and into the meaning of color for the painter. For there before me, huge on the wall, were Frida's definitions of colors. For me, colors were words, verbal images, tropes perhaps, hypertext links to the meanings of colors. When I meant *green,* I spelled it with five letters in English and in Spanish. I used language to stand for green in ways that I did not use language to enact desire. I felt that a poverty of poetry is that it requires no light or its continuous spectrum.

In her own words, Frida explained the meaning of several colors, explaining, for example, blue, green and red: *"Azul: electricidad y pureza amor"; "Verde:*

hojas, tristeza, ciencia, Alemania entera es de este color"; "Rojo: sangre? Pues quien sabe!" I was transfixed, making myself as porous a receptor as I had been standing in the British Museum before the Rosetta Stone or before the Elgin's Marbles of Keats. It seemed to me that this most passionate of painters had sent to me, as I stood there in that present moment, a communiqué from the past, *un recado apasionado,* that would reveal to me the meaning of colors. For after all she was a painter: blue, green, and red were stuff that she got on her hands, made art with, and had to wash off vigorously at the end of the day: acts altogether distinct from mine as a poet who writes the names of colors.

The definition for green struck me as most odd: "Green: leaves, sadness, science, all of Germany is this color." Why? Was it true? Were science and Germany green? Sad? What, I asked myself, did it mean? These definitions sounded poetic to me, so I rationalized that since "Blue: electricity and purity love" had the ring of the lyric, I should be able to make sense. But rationally they meant next to nothing to me. I did not understand. And in truth, there is no reason that a painter's words need make sense. So I forsook understanding and resolved to react. And so I wrote the poem "Letters of Color."

Several years later, Frida Kahlo's diary was published, and once again I was struck with desire and

color

apprehension. The diary is published as a photo reproduction, for it is the diary of an artist and is at least as visual as it is verbal. It is full of color and full of words. I turned to the page of the color definitions and found that I had been mislead. The textual representation at the Mexican Museum had presented her reflections on color as if a dictionary, a list of words defined by synonym, metaphor, explanation. But in the diary, the meaning of color was something quite different. It began by zigzagged lines of two colors followed by the declaration, *"Probaré los lapices tajados al punto infinito que mire siempre adelante,"* I will test the pencils sharpened to the infinite point that always looks forward. And the definitions for blue, green, and red did not begin with the words, the names of the colors, but rather began with the nonverbal blotch, sketch, and smear. There was no word *red* but instead a smear like a thin stain and clots followed by the words, "blood? Well, who knows!" As such, the definitions seemed to read backward, from the weak verbal explanation to the demonstration of color, from name to blotch, from epistemology to ontology.

What I had dismissed in the Mexican Museum as disappointing writing came across in the diary as an attempt to work between media, between meaning in painting and that in poetry, between color and word. There was in the color of the blotch and smear, in the

color

sketch of a leaf and the zigzag line, a presentation that was a thing itself along side the linguistic. In my previous reading of the definitions, I formed an understanding whose fundamental paradigm was the dictionary, which has nothing to do with painting. Seeing her diary pointed out a way that color differed from line and deferred from word as well. But it was the imbrication of color, line, and word that perhaps said most. And this was as missed by my lexicographic conception as it was by the Mexican Museum display and as it is by the English translation appended to the photo-reproduced diary in color and Spanish. In our endeavors to translate, we miss the play set about by Frida Kahlo's hand.

color

In a dark pencil, dark gray, Frida Kahlo wrote, *"nada es negro—realmente nada"*: nothing is black—nothing really. It is a clever irony for the color is in fact not black, but blackish, and more, the final *nada* is underlined in green. This, she tell us, is sadness, science, German. In the play of her interaction of color and word, that nothing is black is empirical, perhaps, or perhaps that nothing really is, is a sad fact. And the line *"electricidad y pureza amor"* is written in blue except for the last word, *love,* which is a very dark brown, the only occurrence of the color on the page. Verbally blue is defined as electricity, purity, and love, but in the play between color and word, *love* is set off, emphasized, perhaps as in hyperbole, perhaps as in asserting its singularity, perhaps in ambiguity. None of this is translatable in text alone, as the poor English translation so well indicates. The English spills over continuously, without the punctuation or trope of color, constructing a sadly pale verbal reading.

By seeing the graphic reproduction of the work of her hand, I came to a different sense of how she meant by color. It is ironic that I think I better expressed this sense of meaning before I saw her diary, in a poem of reaction, than I have in all these paragraphs since.

color

23 echo park

I just got off the phone with Kathleen. I haven't seen or spoken to her for a couple of years. She's producing a television show and needs some video bites about Chicano popular culture. The subject area, lucha libre, is not one of my favorites, so I recommend Harry Gamboa: he is Chicano, as smart an artist as there is, and looks good on camera. He'll do.

I haven't seen Harry in just about as much time, but we've kept in contact: failing to get money for a video project; doing photos; inquiring about the two Barbaras, his daughter's birth and his wife's health. I have known him since after he got kicked out of what was to become the premier Chicano band, Los Lobos, and formed the premier Chicano art group, Asco. I still think he has the most fertile range of any Chicano artist, though I do have to admit that I think no one on this side of the border paints murals like Willie Herron, and that's saying quite a lot. I once participated in a performance piece of Harry's and, covered with black paper, lay down on the Third Street bridge along with a lot of others similarly clad. I owe him this book, for were it not for him and the Goddess Chaos, I'd not have walked the Irish sand when I did, nor begin this work as I do. So, if I can turn him onto a brief television thing, so much the better.

The last time I saw Kathleen we got into a misunderstanding about sex. An actress friend of hers took me to visit Kathleen and Bill, her screenwriting lover. When we got to their house in Echo Park, there were others there as well, three film editors and Kathleen's assistant producer. I was the only non-Hollywood type there, and if you include wannabes, the only one in half the city as well. We ate barbecued fish and vegetables, looked out at the city from the hillside, and carried on conversation, part of which touched on the similarities between Johannesburg and Los Angeles, the segregation and gated communities, all of which was news to me, having never been to South Africa.

Eventually talk turned to violence, and Kathleen mentioned that in the course of her work she saw quite a bit of violent footage. Concerned with what I considered to be an occupational hazard, I asked if she found herself becoming desensitized. After she gave a brief and vague response, I pressed on: had, in fact, her work diminished her passion? With that question, I inadvertently crossed the lines of communication in a most entertaining way. Kathleen was taken aback by my question; Bill, indignant. What business was it of mine, he seemed to ask. I realized at that point that *passion* in Hollywood parlance is something quite different than it is among poets. I continued, pushing for a direct response even though it was clear to all that I was prying into their sex life. I think *passion* is a euphemism in cinema and television for *coitus,* and so to inquire about losing passion is to inquire about losing the ability to climax. It was great fun, and we all left laughing.

echo park

24 beat

Part of the magic of dance is that it resists an essential impossibility through physical acts, through real leaps of faith. As an articulation of the body in rhythm, dance coordinates movement with beat, whether up, down, or off. Beats are read as a pattern, and the body moves rhythmically in dance. The impossibility is simply that dance relies on a faith in rhythm. For while the dancer perceives rhythm as a syntax of beats, rhythm's value for dance lies in its telos, in a pattern projected into the future. Rhythm structures events that do not yet exist.

Dance rests on the projection of rhythm, the sense of which rests on the relation to, and the matter of, time. It is faith, perhaps, faith that a next beat will come to be, that allows rhythm to be realized, and that allows the body to synchronize movement with the beat in the rhythm of dance. Or if not faith, even a weak and naive one, it is physical fact, or if not actual fact, it is practical correlation, that informs the keeping of time and that inspires one's keeping on time in the series of motor and musical events.

Dance configures beats in a sense of rhythm and coordinates body movement in anticipation of rhythmic repetition, but as it does, what is its sense of time? Does the dancer, for example, experience the present instance of each beat in a passage of time, perhaps like an event that punctuates the flow of temporal matter or that moves forward on a line of time? If true and factual that time is the medium upon which rhythm is projected, then is dance, to some degree, not so much the anticipation of actual beats, but the measuring out of identical temporal fragments? Time as such then would be the medium, flow, line, or fabric upon which events, from musical beats to human births, happen. Dance in this sense would constitute movement as an analog to the flow of time and perhaps only secondarily as an expression of beat.

But it is possible to consider dance in the first instance a correlation of movement to beat. Instead of rhythm defined as the organization of time, as musical theorists would have it, rhythm could be considered an organization of events, each beat an event with its own life, each its own whole. Such dance would be structured on the rhythm of events as they transpire, on the lives of whole events, which are not identical bits of perfectly parsed time. The possibility of dance would not be based on the fact, fabric and

beat

flow of time, but on the realization of events, on the occurrence of beats.

A present concern in literary criticism, once again, is the anti-Semitism of T.S. Eliot. Because of his stature and his dominance in modernist poetics, most especially in England, Eliot's prejudices are discussed and apologized for more often than are those of Ezra Pound or Henry James, for example. Eliot, the Missourian who became an "Anglo-Catholic Royalist" "more British than the British" is treated in something of the way that is Shakespeare: his stature nullifies serious accusations of anti-Semitism. It is a tautology applied to a writer essential to the canon: since he is great, he is great or, in a deductive variation, since his work is great art, it must be of great spirit. Eliot's depiction of a Bleistein or Shakespeare's of Shylock cannot be evidence of anti-Semitism, or so the logic goes.

The current reading of Eliot makes a distinction that seems to me similar to the problem of dance. Eliot can be a great artist and an anti-Semite; I find nothing in aesthetic theory or moral philosophy that precludes either. But one can take note of how one reads his anti-Semitism, whether in themes or in bits. The two extremes differ in that one emphasizes the general sense of the flow of meaning while the other emphasizes each literal event, one at a time. Those who emphasize theme read Eliot backwards, from a

beat

general meaning that explains individual events. Such a reading finds that the whole makes sense and makes sense of the constituent parts. To put it musically, the sense of rhythm makes sense of the individual beats.

On the other hand, locating Eliot's anti-Semitism first in the constitutive elements of *The Waste Land,* such as in the etymological, metaphorical, and grammatical bits, emphasizes the construction of meaning along other lines. The individual events of the text come to accrue meaning through syntax, through a logic of synecdoche and sequence. The lack of capitalizing jew or the etymology of Bleistein can be identified as fragments in the logic of Eliot's anti-Semitism, or can they? Critics of this reading of Eliot often argue that each such poetic event, on its own, is benign and can appear prejudicial only to those so predisposed to finding anti-Semitism.

In a nonpoetic example of the syntax of prejudice, the video tape of the LAPD beating of Rodney King broke down the movement of racism into its individual beats. On behalf of the police assailants, Stacey Koon and Laurence Powell, the defense attorneys slowed the video tape to its individual still frames, down to the individual events of the beating. They then challenged the jury to identify the exact instance of the violation of civil rights. The defense insisted that at no individual beat in the dance of police violence was it possible to identify a rhythm or theme of

beat

racism. After an acquittal and the LA riots, Koon and Powell were subsequently convicted of the lesser crime of denying civil rights. The defense for racist beating or anti-Semitic writing is that the individual beat need not participate in a rhythm.

In the end, it is not the passage of time or the freezing of time that matters so much in the story of a beating: each nightstick blow hurt with each individual strike, and the sequence of blows by white LAPD officers on a fallen Rodney King beat out a pattern, beat out a racist rhythm. The story of racism is a series of beatings, blow by blow in a rhythm whose theme is dominance. The dance of power, the movement of bodies to administer violence in the single beat as well as in rhythm, is a dominance that mystifies. Racism has no time. It is a pattern of beatings here.

beat

25 life

Last night I drove to the Mission District to attend a benefit, and as I write this I am listening to a recording of "Desapareciones" by Los Fabulosos Cadillacs. I listen to the lyrics by Rubén Blades and recall the lyric last night by Lorna Dee Cervantes, and I write now, I know, about the end. Lorna read a poem about a very particular ending, about a moment now approaching two decades past, when San José police shot Danny Treviño, killing him as he sat unarmed in his car. Lorna's rhetorical trick brings Danny before us, alive by the will of the poem. This is what Rubén Blades does in his salsa lyrics: he bears witness and testifies and vivifies the dead by singing his canto of recollection.

The event last night was to forestall an end: the artist Yolanda López is gravely ill, and the artistic community gathered to show their love and to raise money for her treatment. A particular pallor was cast over the event because José Antonio Burciaga was unable to make the drive up from Monterey, being too consumed by his own battle with cancer. And a momentary scare for us was the news that José Montoya had had a stroke, but his appearance belied the fact: he was there to read and looked as ready as ever. Up until Ricardo Sánchez succumbed to cancer a year ago, the community of Chicano poets had not had to deal with the facts of our demise: we were all alive. In fact until Sánchez died, all the veterano poets who had given voice and form to a Chicano consciousness and to the homeland, Aztlán, were alive and writing and therefore, it seemed to us, so was the movement. Our moment of Chicano Renaissance is like the prime moments of other locations, Harlem and Paris in the 20s and 30s, Madrid and Florence in 1492.

Even though the event wasn't a funeral, it took on one aspect of the Chicano version of the death ritual: the celebration of life. We affirmed the good for Yolanda and Tony and for ourselves as well. That evening the Mission Cultural Center was the place for us to touch, dar abrazos, to catch up on the changes in our lives, and to talk, laugh, and dance. Cherrié's baby and Lorna's baby had transformed into little boys. Juan Felipe had a new book out and was going to be at Cal in the winter. Francisco had finished his series of Spanish text books. Rose was quitting San Francisco State for the life of the writer. And José was hanging in, looking bad in his tando, el mero jefe del tribu casindio. Charley, Margarita, and I chanced upon a random photo-op, having unwittingly dressed similarly: black shirts, khaki green pants.

In *"Desapareciones,"* Rubén Blades proclaims the names and the quotidian details of life that become the frantically held links with the desaparecidos, those people kidnapped, tortured, and made to disappear by the governments in places like Guatemala and Argentina. One woman pleads for information about her husband Ernesto who was last seen wearing *camisa oscura y pantalon claro.* Someone else has spent three days searching for a sister, Altagracia, who last *salió del trabajo para la escuela.* The son of another, Agustín, is a medical student, *un buen muchacho although es aveces terco cuando opina.* In *"El padre Antonio y el monaguillo Andrés,"* his song about the assassination of Bishop Romero in El Salvador, Blades details not only the life of the Bishop, but that of Andrés, the altar boy, who was killed as well, noting for example his love of soccer.

For Lorna, the telling of the murder of Danny Treviño is personal, another poem that she fashioned from a life surrounded by violence in San José's Barrio Horseshoe. Charley Trujillo responds to the poem as to another version of a familiar story. Charley writes novels about his experience in Vietnam and lectures about violence there and on the home front. He reminds me that the San José police killed Danny's cousin, Tomás Treviño, as well, shooting him fifteen times as he stood in his own kitchen. Both Lorna and Charley had gone to support Yolanda, and both have been close to Tony Burciaga for a long time.

Of all the people there for Yolanda, Lorna has been my friend for the longest time. I actually met José Montoya earlier but did not get to know him for quite a while. And Juan Felipe was in my mind way, way back: when a group of Chicanos first brought Alurista out to New York, the poet of the homeland raved about this great poet back in San Diego. But I've worked with Lorna almost since I first moved to San José. I remember being at San José City College and having a student tell me that this poet lived across the freeway. This was back in the days when she was working on *Mango.*

I remember when I met Lorna thinking her much like a small black bird, the kind that I'd see on my lawn. This was before *Emplumada,* and she seemed to me as fragile a creature as she was sure a poet. But after the publication of the first book she shed any real fragility and grew to something else. The end of one thing, the change to something else. A fact and trick of life.

When I came to Berkeley, three consecutive school years began marked by tragedy. In 1989 there was the 7.1 Loma Prieta earthquake: the Bay Bridge down, 62 dead. In 1991 there was the fire in the hills behind campus: 2843 houses gone, 26 dead. In between in 1990 there was the scene at Henry's: hostages, a schizophrenic driven by voices, sexual assault, and two deaths. Henry's was one in a series of fatal fall passages for Cal students, and this in a period of trauma in a state of trauma: 6 years of drought, the

LA riots, fires, floods, the 6.7 in LA, and all of this be-
sides the regular deaths by mud slides or shootings
and the dehydration of "aliens" lost in the desert.

My own small world had been rocked as well: di-
vorce, a daughter's running away with a Ukrainian
DJ, the break up of my family, and racism on the job
front. My bid for tenure in English at Cal had turned
to an ugly display of discrimination and retaliation,
beginning immediately after my public reading of
"Tomorrow Today," a poem criticizing the Univer-
sity's opposition to affirmative action. These are ugly
times for Chicanos at the University of California,
and victories like those of Rudy Acuña are few and
extremely hard fought. Yet throughout this, it is the
personal element of our struggle, the individuals who
take stands as well as those who acquiesce in fear,
that renders our efforts so human. It is clear to us that
our struggle is not always victorious: Cecilia
Burciaga, for example, was forced from her position
at Stanford. The personal dimension of that struggle
meant that Tony Burciaga would leave Stanford too.
He was an artist-in-residence and painted the *Last
Supper of Chicano Heroes* mural there, but he left
with his wife when she took a position in Monterey.
And eventually after that, and after the moment that
I began writing this piece, in another struggle in the
future, cancer would kill Tony. The comic and critical
poet would be gone. I have a video tape I made in
1980 of Tony and Lorna. He reads *"Letanía en caló,"*
and she reads "Beneath the Shadow of the Freeway."

It is a testimony to the times and equally one to the spirit of the individual poets. I like the tape because it is a personal statement, theirs as well as mine, a statement to the testimony of life.

When I met my class after the killings at Henry's, I stood before the large group realizing that they looked to me to make sense of the daze. My job was to profess sense, to derive meaning from event. The place they used to meet at to drink and laugh had been turned into a place of horror by Mirdad Dashdi's insane and suicidal acts. Friends and classmates had been taken hostage, assaulted sexually, shot, and one killed. It was a particularly human violence, more personal than the earthquake the year before or the fire yet to come. I had nothing to say, almost nothing except to address the situation, to put words to the event, to bear witness and to testify in the present for the sake of our recollection. I suggested that we go and celebrate life. I did not suggest how; each student, I was sure, would have a private and personal vision. For my sake, I think it best to hold another human whom one loves.

My students left to talk with each other outside in the bright light of day. A community of Chicano poets came together for a sick artist. I have records, electronic and in memory, of testimony by Rubén Blades, Tony Burciaga, and Lorna Dee Cervantes. It is right to sympathize and right to struggle. And it is right to celebrate the living amid the killing.

110

life

zero

Mexicans invented zero. And Mexicans were better markers of time than Europeans. In the Aztec calendar, after eighteen months of twenty days, the year ended with a vague period of five days. It was a time of chaos.

Zero time and chaos are my birthright. They are the conditions of my story, the notes of my lyric, the beats of my rhythm. I finish this book now outside numerical order, in this coda, recalling what I can just imagine.

It began during an impossibility of place, one of those instances where my daughters and I were in different times, facing different directions, and seeing in different light. I left Mireya asleep in Dublin alone on the island. I had stayed as long as I could, but the events conspired to have me leave for Italy. We had rehearsed schedules and alternative plans the evening before and had driven the Opel around in the dark to acquaint her with Connolly Station. I left early, first for London, then Milan. It was cold summer, wet.

Marisol was somewhere over North America, taking the polar route, perhaps a jet stream, east, aiming for Ireland. Her departure had changed and been changed over and over again, and neither Mireya nor I would believe that she had actually taken off until we saw her in Ireland. Xóchitl was somewhere in California. In a week she and I were to rendezvous at Heathrow and take green Aer Lingus to Dublin. These girls who mean so much to me seemed to me then like fragile balls tossed in the air at once, in flight, arcing, gliding, falling on their own beyond my sight.

Mireya met Marisol at the airport and proudly took control. The sixteen year old had a couple hundred Irish punts in her pocket and would introduce her older sister to the island and lead her to our place in Sligo. She tells me the trip went fine, the only slight mishap was taking the less comfortable train north: more smoke, less space. But this had been a conscious choice, so as to get home a bit earlier. Marisol, she says, slept the way: taxi, train, taxi. And her directions to the driver in Sligo town took them without hitch to our place by the sea, past Lissadell, between Ballyconnell and Cloughboley, at the crossroads, the fairy path, and the wild yellow irises.

While I was in Italy, they went out for a walk: I can see them. Their choices were north and west, towards Dermot and Helen's and the cliffs; west and north, toward Roskeeragh, the cold flat beach with the black slugs; south, past the well toward Ellen's; or east, past the yellow flowers toward Dunlevy's. It was warmer than it had been; they set off away from the sea, toward the farthest destination, Dunlevy's market. At the crossroads they turned left, passed the fairy path, and followed the road lined with flowers, cows, and piles of stones with the memory of homes. Eventually, after passing the slight rise a couple of miles out, they could see Ben Bulben in the horizon. The high, flat mountain was the prime marker for Co Sligo, navigationally and spiritually, but from our house it could not be seen. Its sight marked distance from home and signaled that Dunlevy's might be near.

They bought something at the market, maybe a Solero, perhaps the modeling clay, I really couldn't say, I wasn't with them. Their return, they decided, would take them past Ellen's, in a round about, alternate way. They ended up missing the turn, it being a place, after all, where the roads have no names and look similar to newly arrived urban types. They ended up at Raghly by the German castle and tried to head back in the general direction north across the fields and the bog and the megaliths. For hours Ben Bulben remained visible: clearly they were nowhere near home.

What did they see then? Who had walked in the same bog millennia before? What lay buried in the preserving earth under their purview? At points across the bog, each of their steps must have been

physically difficult; they must have thought them-
selves as lost as they were, cut off from origin and des-
tination as well. When would their trek end, a matter
of hours at most, they hoped. Beneath their feet, the
bog of a small island where grew wild yellow irises,
and where a well in tall bush hid somewhere not far.
And in the distance were farmers and herdsmen and
the detritus of a people once twice as numerous.

When Xóchitl and I did drive up days later in the
Volkswagen Golf, we were greeted by a fire of coal
and peat. Dermot and Helen had dropped off dried
slices of the bog for us to burn. Mireya and Marisol
noted the ease with which we had arrived and related
the tale of a long, long walk across a bog.

Coco Fusco tells me that she is leaving for Chiapas.
I tell her that as soon as I put down the last period to
this thing I'm writing, I'm taking off for Guerrero.
Perhaps, we muse, one of us will run into Marcos or
Lucio. Our talk turns to Mexican cinema and two of
our favorite icons, Tin Tan and Tongolele. Marisol, I
tell Coco, at two or three years of age used to repeat-
edly declare, "I'm Tongolele."

One thing Chicanos have contributed to human-
ity is a sense of border. We walk and swim and get lost
and find ourselves and make life there in zero time
and chaos.

Tentli

Tentli–s. labio; pico de ave; hocico de ani-
mal; orilla de algo; fig. memoria, recuerdo,
tira de escritura.

Think of the mouth as port of desire,
an edge that marks thought from
sky and the flight of birds. Want across
dreams recalled days after, desire itself
written like past motion in light.
Lip is edge, the border demarking in light
and in light of day, desire is that edge,
that border, trim and light. Had we but
edge equal to desire, bound by our simple
plans and steps of desire. Bound by our
binds of brave blows, destruction for
certain, mouth of such desire, mouth
of sex and the sex of sex, had we but
the motion at edge to take bright
time, brave motion, and destroy
some center in its cool repose.

Amor y caos

Antes, el día antes, habían las cosas,
horas de cosas, reglas, y máquinas.
Nací, lo sé por la lógica griega
y por el orden de la historia de hombre.
Antes, el día antes, tuve yo una vida,
debe ser, y tuve momentos, llamas
verdes, azules, y una fé, tuve fé.
¿Porqué los libros, fotos y las huellas,
sino pruebas del diccionario, sino
del paso perdido de cristo, sino
la linea quebrada que llega hasta tí?
Se dice que antes existían cosas,
la muralla de minutos, fil de horas;
un sueño lleno, dicen mis amigos,
existía antes de que te conocí.
Antes no había nada.
En tus ojos no nací aquel momento
ni en tu vista comenzó mi vida allá,
pero después, un día después, cayó

el pasado a pedazos, a pedazos.
No dudo ni creo yo:
Antes, el día antes, habían las cosas,
y antes no había nada.
En tu vista verde de caos, ando,
en tu respiro mi paso de nuevo,
en tus dedos de minutos el tiempo.
Quebrado al momento ando,
suelto de la significación, la ley,
aquí en la detalla clara de tu ser.

Driving in Fog

She breaks silent, "Asina
es perder el alma," gives voice
once. This is how it feels, driving
in fog. What time is it after all
to lose one's soul may be what
she felt but just asked, "¿Qué
horas son?" What if you run off
into the fog and I never see you
again, even as I stop and peer? What
if I want so much to touch your skin?
If the sound of heavy wind is all
we'll ever hear, if there is nothing
beyond an edge, just beyond
our sight? Does it creep into the car
interior, so diffuse up close I don't
see it fog the windshield with its
thinnest of membranes?
The point about fog is that this
muffled obfuscation is swirling, top
quarks of fog set loose, decaying, and

it matters not whether we know this,
fog is now only and will never be.
Whether gift, blessing or sign: it is fog.
It is not as the Russians believe,
not like flying diaphanous in deep air.
I am driving in fog. Where are you beside

Cover photograph and decorative device by Mireya
Arteaga. Editorial production by Kirsten Janene-
Nelson. Designed and typeset in Futura and
Sabon by Thomas Christensen at Mercury
House, San Francisco, June 1997.
Printed and bound by
Hignell Printing on
acid-free paper.